An English Heritage Handbook

Richmond Castle

Yorkshire

by the late

SIR CHARLES PEERS CBE, D Litt, MA, FBA, FSA

formerly Chief Inspector of Ancient Monuments

LONDON : HISTORIC BUILDINGS AND
MONUMENTS COMMISSION FOR ENGLAND

Contents

Previously published by HMSO 1981
First published by HBMCE 1985

Published by the Historic Buildings and Monuments Commission for England and printed in England by BPCC Ltd., Derby. Dd 714500 C120 3/85

ISBN 1 85074 005 4

Owners of the castle

The position of Richmond Castle is so strong by nature and at the same time so suitable for habitation, that it would be no wonder if traces of prehistoric occupation were to be found there. But, as far as we know, early man made no use of the site, and it is not until after the Norman Conquest that the definite history of Richmond begins. It was granted, with other lands of its former Saxon owner, to Alan the Red, son of Eudes, Count of Penthièvre, and he is said to have begun building the castle here in 1071. Fifteen years later it is set down in Domesday Book as part of the land of Earl Alan, but Gilling and Catterick, not Richmond, are the principal places of the district. The earliest mention of the name Richmond appears to date from 1090, when the archdeaconry of Richmond is referred to; its origin is not certainly known. The town must soon have begun to spring up round the castle, as the parish church was a large building in the twelfth century; it seems at first to have relied for its protection on the castle, and not until 1312, as a precaution against Scottish raids, did it obtain a stone wall of its own.

The Saxon owner, at the time of the Conquest, of the lands which became the Honour of Richmond, was Edwin, Earl of Mercia, and he seems to have been left in possession at any rate till 1068, when he took part in the rising of that year. He died in 1071, the date usually given for the grant of his lands to Alan the Red; it is possible that he remained in possession till his death.

Alan the Red was the first Norman holder of the Honour of Richmond, though this name of the fief does not occur till more than a century later. He was related to the reigning Duke of Brittany, and this connection, which often caused his successors to be subjects of the King of England and the King of France at the same time, was a fruitful source of trouble and of the forfeiture of lands for three hundred years.

Alan held Richmond from 1071 to 1089, and it is probable that the early masonry of the curtain walls dates from his time. Two of his brothers succeeded him, Alan the Black in 1089 and Stephen, Count of Penthièvre in 1093. Stephen's son, Alan, held Richmond 1137–46, and by his marriage with Bertha, daughter and heiress of Conan III, Duke of Brittany, brought the Honour of Richmond into close connection with the duchy. His son, Conan the Little, Earl of Richmond 1146–71, inherited the dukedom of Brittany in 1164, but found it prudent to betroth his infant daughter Constance to Geoffrey of Anjou, son of King Henry II, in 1166, and to resign the duchy to the King. Conan married Margaret, sister of King Malcolm IV of Scotland, and their daughter, Constance, was nine years old at his death in 1171. Henry II as her guardian kept the Honour of Richmond in his hands till after her marriage with Geoffrey in 1181. Geoffrey died in 1186, leaving a son, Arthur, and a daughter, Eleanor, and his widow seems to have held the Honour of Richmond till her death in 1201, when her third husband, Guy de Thouars, was left as tenant of the Honour. Arthur, son of Constance and Geoffrey, was murdered by King John in 1203, and Guy de Thouars, taking arms against the King, forfeited Richmond in 1204. The Honour was granted to Robert de Beaumont, Earl of Leicester; the castle, however, seems to have remained in the hands of the Crown. Robert died soon after receiving the grant and the Honour likewise lapsed to the Crown. In 1205 it was granted to Ralph de Blundeville, Earl of Chester, who had been Constance's second husband from 1187 to 1197, when the marriage was annulled. Constance had left two daughters by her third marriage, and the elder of these married Peter de Braine, who became Duke of Brittany and received a grant of part of the Honour of Richmond in 1218, part, however, remaining with the the Earl of Chester. The double allegiance which Peter thus owed in respect of his English and French lands soon brought him into difficulties. In 1223 Richmond was temporarily confiscated by Henry III for default of military service in Wales, and again in 1224 for fighting for France against England in Poitou. But the Duke of Brittany was too useful an ally to the English King against France to be lightly discarded, and his English Honours were soon restored to him. In 1225, King Henry even proposed to marry Duke Peter's daughter, Yolande, in return for help against the French, but in 1227 Yolande was betrothed to Louis IX's brother, John, and in consequence her father's share of Richmond was again forfeited and granted to the Earl of Chester. In 1230 it came back to the duke once more, but in 1234, having to make a definite choice between his English and French allegiance, he submitted to Louis IX, and so finally lost Richmond, dying in 1250 without recovering it.

The Honour was granted to Peter of Savoy in 1240 and he held it till 1266, when he restored it to the Duke of Brittany, whose son and heir, John, had married Beatrice, daughter of Henry III, in 1260. John, succeeding his father, had to choose between England and France in 1294, and siding with France was deprived of Richmond by Edward I. He was, however, reinstated in 1298 and died in 1305, and in 1306 the King gave Richmond to his second son, John. John II died in 1334, and Richmond went to his nephew, John III, Duke of Brittany, who held it till his death in 1341.

In 1342 John of Gaunt, son of King Edward III, was created Earl of Richmond, and held Richmond till 1372, when he became King of Castile. John of Montfort, Duke of Brittany, then had a grant of the earldom, but the double allegiance involved him in the usual difficulties. In 1381 he lost his earldom for doing homage to the French King, Charles V, and, though the revenues were restored to him in 1384, they were forfeited in the same year on account of an alliance he had made with France. Richmond was then given by Richard II to his Queen, Anne of Bohemia, and after her death it was leased to Ralph Nevill, Lord of Raby. The last link in the long connection with Brittany was the grant of the Honour in 1398 to Joan, sister of the then duke, who used the style of Earl of Richmond in 1399.

In the same year, however, Henry IV granted the Honour to Ralph Nevill, Earl of Westmorland. John, Duke of Bedford, a son of that King, held the Honour and Earldom from 1425 to his death 1435, when they reverted to the Crown. Henry VI made a partial grant of the castle to Richard

Nevill, Earl of Salisbury, about 1450 but the Honour was held by the King's half-brother, Edmund Tudor, as Earl of Richmond, from 1453 to his death in 1456. He left a son, Henry Tudor, who afterwards became Henry VII.

Edward IV gave the Honour and castle of Richmond to his brother George, Duke of Clarence, in 1462; on his execution in 1478, Richard, Duke of Gloucester, succeeded him and continued to hold Richmond after his accession as Richard III. Henry Tudor, however, styled himself Earl of Richmond as heir of his father Edmund, and with his accession in 1485 as Henry VII, the Honour merged in the Crown.

The title was used by Henry VIII, when in 1525 he created his natural son, Henry Fitzroy, Duke of Richmond; the dukedom lapsed at his death in 1536 at the age of seventeen, but was revived in 1623 in favour of Ludovic Stuart, who died in the same year, and again in favour of James Stuart, Earl of Lennox, in 1641. Charles, fifth Duke of Richmond, died in 1672, and in 1675 Charles II conferred the dukedom on his natural son Charles Lennox, with whose descendants it still remains.

History

It is at first sight strange that a castle which has been the chief place of the great Honour of Richmond, and the possession of so many royal and powerful owners, should have played so inconsiderable a part in the history of the nation. Its position, however, is away from the important lines of communication and though in itself very strong, commands little beyond the entrance to Swaledale, and is hemmed in on three sides by the high moors. A Roman road, in part called Leeming Lane, running along the western edge of the plain of York, passes through Catterick about 6 miles (9.7km) to the east of Richmond, and another Roman road branching off from the first between Catterick and Aldborough, and running north-west through Bowes into Cumbria, passed at about the same distance to the north, but close to Gilling, the headquarters of Earl Edwin of Mercia.

It would seem that Earl Alan, in leaving Gilling for Richmond, was more concerned to find a defensible site for his castle than one which was in easy communication with the outside world. This is borne out by the statement in the fourteenth-century register referred to later (page 9), that Earl Alan built his castle to protect his own men against the attacks of the English, who were then everywhere dispossessed, and likewise against those of the Danes. As a result Richmond Castle had little strategic value, and save for possible Scottish raids saw little fighting; the Wars of the Roses and the Civil War alike passed it by. It appears in history as the prison of King William the Lion of Scotland, taken at Alnwick in 1174, and King John in the last year of his reign ordered that the castle should be destroyed, if it could not be held against his enemies. Evidently the order was not carried out, but the result of the comparative unimportance of Richmond is seen in the words of an inquest taken in 1341 after the death of John III, Duke of Brittany. The castle is there said to be worth nothing in yearly return 'within the walls or in the ditch,' and to be much in want of repair in buildings and walls. Clearly the expense of its upkeep was grudged, as not repaying the outlay. A survey taken in 1538 shows that the whole castle was then in decay and a great deal of it roofless: Leland, about 1540, plainly calls it a 'mere ruine.' In spite of all this, it remains today one of large extent and in some ways of much more than usual interest. Setting aside such exceptional buildings as the White Tower in the Tower of London, and the great Tower of Colchester Castle, no other castle in England can show so much masonry belonging to the first twenty years or so after the Norman Conquest. Its great hall is the oldest building of its kind in Britain except perhaps that at Chepstow Castle, and its great tower, though far from being in the first rank for size, has such advantages of site and proportion as to make it at least the equal in dignity of any other in England. It is recorded in the register of the Honour of Richmond that Conan the Little, 1146–71,

View from the southwest

built this tower, but though he may have begun it, the Pipe Roll for 18 Henry II (i.e. 1172, the eighteenth year of the reign of Henry II) shows that it was at least finished by the King, during the time that he held the castle as guardian of Conan's daughter, Constance. In 1172 £51-11-3d was spent on the work of the houses and tower of Richmond, and in 1175 £30-6-8d on the castle and its houses. With the exception of Scolland's Hall, most of the masonry now remaining on the south or river front of the castle is of twelfth-century date, and may be Henry's work, and the gateway and walls of the cockpit, as the eastern ward is named, are equally of his time.

In 1278 John I of Brittany and Beatrice his wife, daughter of Henry III, received a confirmation of their grant of lands to the yearly value of £25 for the support of six chaplains from Egglestone Abbey, who were to say mass in the greater chapel of the castle for the souls of John and Beatrice. These chaplains, who were White Canons, were to live in an enclosed place on the west side of the castle, near the greater chapel.

Edward I, who had the castle in his hands from 1294–98, gave orders for its repair and safekeeping in 1297, and Duke John I, to whom the castle was restored in 1298, or more probably his son, John II, 1306-34, built the great chamber and a chapel against the east curtain wall, adjoining Scolland's Hall on the north east. The upper parts of the Robin Hood and Gold Hole Towers, with what remains of the wall walk between them along the east curtain, are of the same date, as is the vault inserted in the ground storey of the great tower.

The building of three additional towers is recommended in the survey of 1538, one on the north side of the cockpit and two against the west curtain wall, but there is no evidence that they were ever built, and in the same survey there is mention of the failure of several parts of the walls, which has since then done such great damage to the castle. From this time it would seem that the castle was left to decay, and the progress of its ruin may be gauged by a comparison of the Buck drawings of 1720–30, now in the Sutherland Collection in the Bodleian Library, with the Buckler drawings of 1816 in the British Museum.

In 1732, Mr Wharton, agent to the Duke of Richmond, made some excavations in the barbican and discovered the moat and drawbridge, but they were again covered over. In 1761 and the three following years some £350 was spent in repairing the castle. The lower part of the great tower had been much robbed of its masonry so that the wall faces overhung as shown on the Bucks' drawings; the walls were made up to their original face, and the battlements and parapets on the top of the tower restored. The dilapidated walls of the cockpit and other parts were repaired or rebuilt from the foundations where the old work had fallen away. It is recorded that the mortar was mixed with soot to assimilate the better with the old parts of the building.

During the nineteenth century the castle was greatly disfigured by the building of a long barrack building on the west side of the great court, and the fitting up of the great tower as a place for military stores. By levelling up the east side of the great court a mass of earth was piled against the east curtain wall, which was already in a failing condition; the second court, or cockpit, was cut up into allotment gardens and the area outside the eastern wall was disfigured with pigsties, chicken runs and rubbish heaps.

When the castle came into the care of the nation in 1910, a systematic scheme of clearing and repair was begun and continued for many years. The repair of the east curtain has been the most difficult and costly part of the work. The rocky promontory on which the castle stands falls away steeply here and the foundations are not carried down to the rock. A section of the strata shows that under the surface soil is a bed of brown clay, 9ft (2.7m) thick, resting on 5ft (1.5m) of blue clay. Under this is gravel, 8ft (2.4m) thick, on more brown clay. These beds follow the slope of the ground with a quick fall eastwards, and the natural drainage of the great court takes the same line. In the result the subsoil is constantly wet, and the clay has slid eastwards carrying the wall with it. Northward from the abutment of the north wall of the cockpit, which has acted as a buttress, the eleventh-century curtain has bulged outwards in a great curve, being dangerously tilted forward at the same time, while the contemporary tower at this point has cracked away from the curtain and fallen, and its base is now some 6ft (1.8m) further down the slope than when it was built. The precise date of the fall of the tower is not easy to fix. It was evidently standing in 1538, as were two towers in the cockpit, and one on the south side of the great court, which have now completely disappeared.

The buildings

At the time of the Conquest the typical Norman fortification was the motte-and-bailey castle. This in its simplest form consisted of a large earthen mound or motte, with a bailey or courtyard attached to it, enclosed by an earthen bank. Ditches, wet or dry, surrounded the earthwork, and for further strength wooden palisades were set on the bank and round the top of the motte. By such means a site of no natural strength can be made into a very defensible stronghold, but at Richmond the circumstances suggested a widely different scheme of fortification, and it seems that neither motte nor banks ever existed here. Stone abounded on the site and masonry walls formed part of the earliest defences. The triangular platform which was chosen as the site of the castle was sufficiently protected on the south by the banks of the Swale, but on the other two sides of the triangle massive stone walls were built, the principal entrance to the castle being through a gatehouse at the apex of the triangle on the north. Three rectangular towers projected from the east curtain wall; in the west curtain there seems to have been only one tower at the southwest angle. A little to the north of this tower a wide semicircular arch in the wall marks the position of the castle chapel, the *capella major* mentioned in 1278; the *capella minor* of Earl Alan's time being doubtless that in the ground storey of the northernmost tower in the east curtain, dedicated in honour of St Nicholas. It was presumably the first of these two chapels that Earl Alan granted to the Lastingham monks after he had given them a place at York in which to settle.

The hall and living rooms with kitchens and offices were in the southeast of the great court; there were probably wooden buildings elsewhere against the curtains which have left no remains. Whether the second court, the cockpit, formed part of the eleventh-century castle is uncertain but, if so, it must have been defended by wooden palisades only. In the same way, there is no evidence of masonry defences along the south side of the great court, and wooden palisades may have been set up here also.

In addition to the principal entrance there were three others opening to the great court, one in the east curtain, close to the Robin Hood Tower, one at the southeast angle, and one in the west curtain, at the point where the greater chapel must have stood.

The twelfth-century additions to the castle, all belonging to the second half of the century, were the keep or great tower built over the original gatehouse, the barbican and its gatehouses, the range of buildings along the south front from Scolland's Hall westwards, and the wall enclosing the cockpit, with two towers on it. Nearly all other work belongs to the first half of the fourteenth century, and includes the buildings attributed to Duke John II of Brittany. By a singular piece of good fortune a drawing of the castle, which must date from about the middle of the fourteenth century, is still extant in a MS Register of

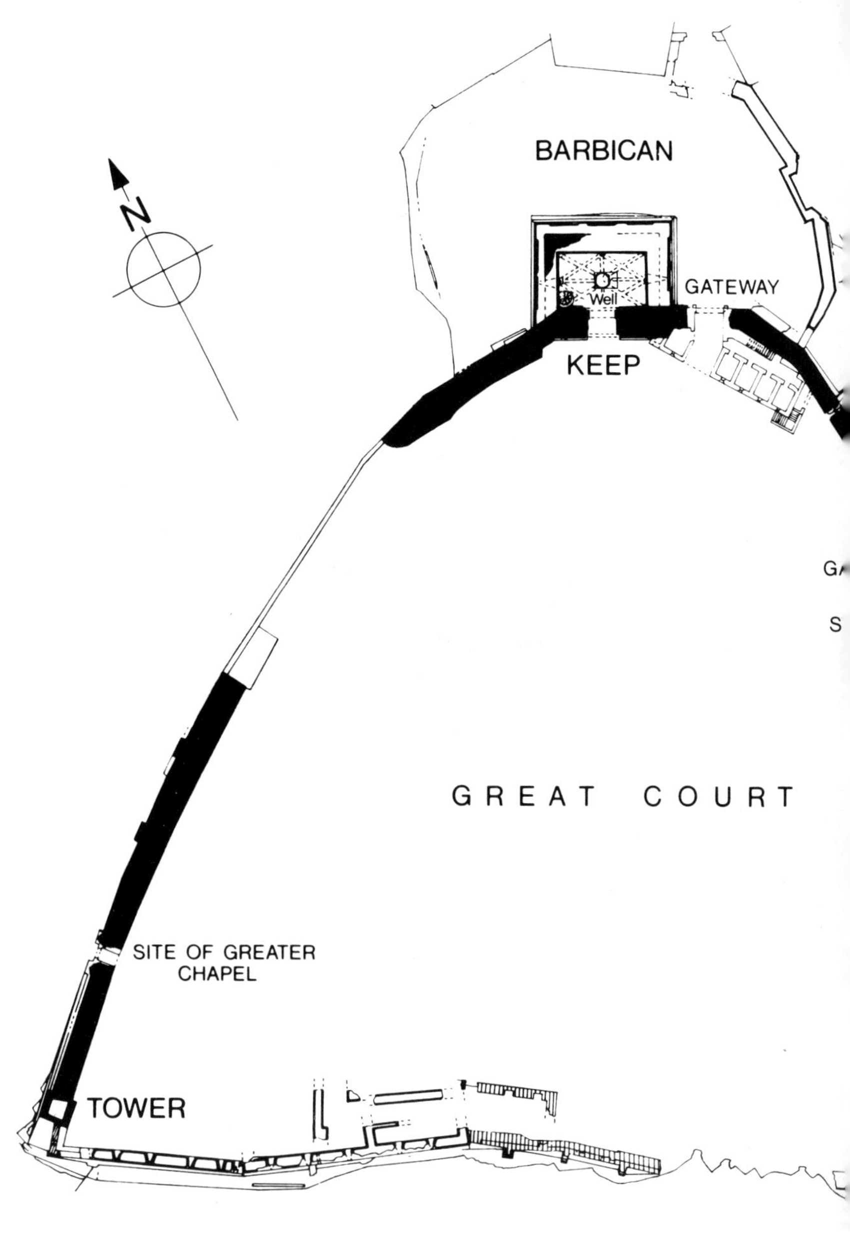
N
BARBICAN
Well
GATEWAY
KEEP
GREAT COURT
SITE OF GREATER
CHAPEL
TOWER

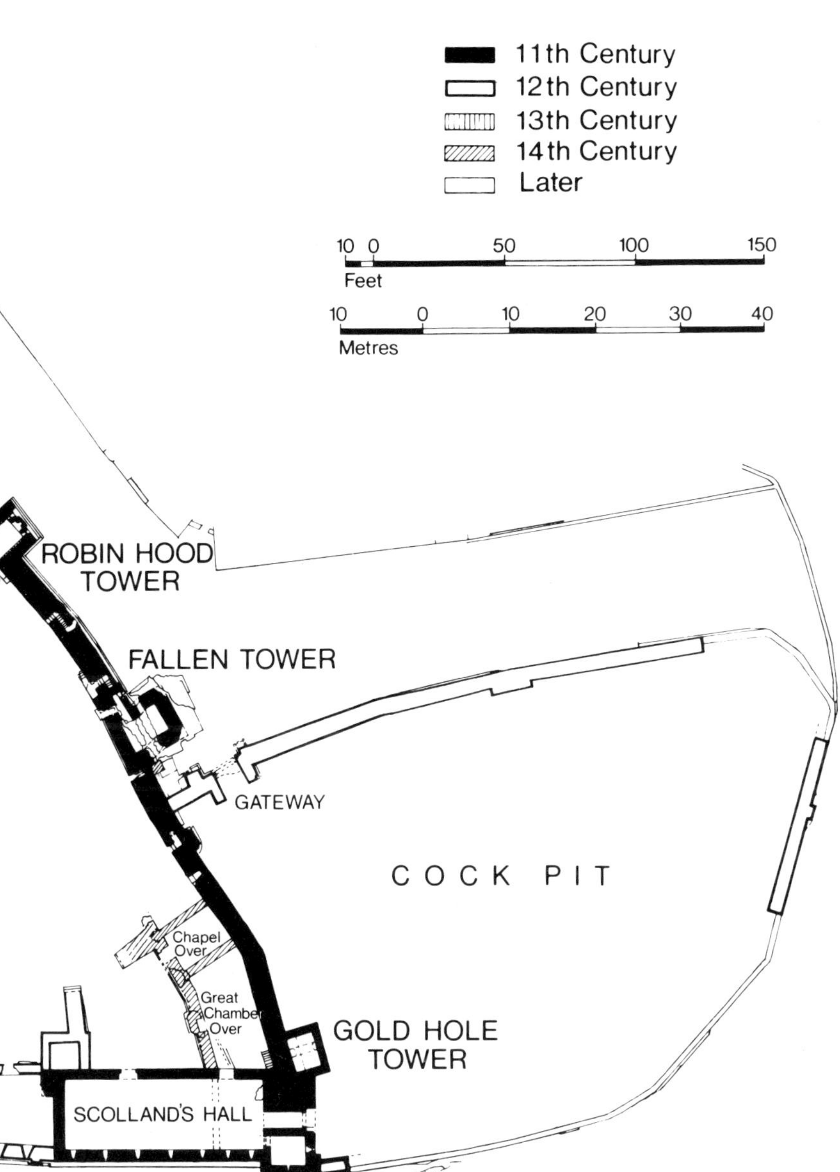
11th Century
12th Century
13th Century
14th Century
Later
10 0 50 100 150
Feet
10 0 10 20 30 40
Metres
ROBIN HOOD TOWER
FALLEN TOWER
GATEWAY
COCK PIT
Chapel Over
Great Chamber Over
GOLD HOLE TOWER
SCOLLAND'S HALL

the Honour of Richmond in the British Museum (Cott Faustina B VII). It was made as a diagram to show the parts of the castle in which the service of castle guard was to be performed by the holders of lands or offices under the Earl of Richmond, but allowing for certain conventions is a quite recognisable view of the castle from the north. The arms of the different persons referred to are blazoned on or near the buildings where their duties were to be performed. The barbican with its gateway, drawbridge, flanking towers and embattled walls is in the foreground, and the ditch is indicated by a watercourse painted blue, although the moat can never have held water. Behind the barbican rises the great tower with its corner turrets and battlements and on it are two shields, *sable a saltire or* and *barry or and gules*. These are referred to in the text as 'The place of the Constable in the enclosure of the Tower (*in claustro turris*)' and 'The place of Conan FitzElias next to the enclosure of the tower on the east side outside the wall.'

East of the great tower is the gateway and portcullis and the east curtain wall with two rectangular towers, between which is a banner *indented fessewise azure and or* marking 'The place of Ralph FitzRobert in the Castle of Richmond near the chapel of St Nicholas.' The start of the walls of the cockpit is shown, enclosing a garden with fruit trees and a round tower meant for the existing Gold Hole Tower, near which is a shield *argent a cross engrailed sable* marking 'The place of the Chamberlain on the east of Scoulandhall next the oven.' Adjoining the tower on the west is Scolland's Hall, the great hall of the castle, with a gabled roof and embattled parapet. Two windows of the hall are shown and its doorway with the steps leading up to it; also its basement with a doorway and one narrow window. The great chamber and chapel to the northeast of the hall are not shown, perhaps for the sake of clearness, as they probably existed at the time. Above the leaded roof of the hall is a banner *barry or and gules* 'The place of Brian FitzAlan in the Great Hall of Scoulande.' To the west is part of the embattled south curtain wall with a banner *azure three chevrons interlaced and a chief or* 'The place of Ralph FitzHenry to the west of Scoulandhall.' Then comes a square building of one storey with a hipped roof, which if it were not for the next entry might be taken for the kitchen; behind it is the roof of a tower on the wall. A little further westward are two small gabled buildings standing near the curtain, and between them a banner *vair a fess gule*, for 'The place of Torphin FitzRobert of Manfeld between the Kitchen and brewhouse.' Next comes a larger gabled building with a leaded roof, a three-light east window, a north door and a west turret and close to it a square tower by which is a shield *argent on a fess sable three bezants* 'The place of Thomas de Burgh on the west of the greater Chapel of the canons on the walls.' From this point the west curtain is shown running northward to the great tower. Except that the arrangement of the buildings against the south curtain is difficult to square with the existing remains, this drawing is of the greatest value for the identification of the various parts of the castle.

A second and more detailed description of the castle is to be found in 'The vewe and staytte of the Castell of Richemonde taken by John Lorde Scrope of Bolton ande Cristofer Lorde Conyers Comyssioners appoynted to vewe the same' in 1538. Everything was in very bad repair at the time, and the wholesale renewals of timber and lead which are recommended suggest that some towers were actually roofless. The survey begins at the outer gatehouse 'callede the porter's loge' with its gates and drawbridge, and passing through the inner gatehouse describes the east curtain and its two towers, then takes the north wall of the cockpit up to 'the est corner towardes the watter of Swaille' where a third tower then stood, which has now perished. A fourth tower, also now vanished, was somewhere on the south side of the cockpit; the wall from this tower to the southeast angle of the great court was 'in decay and moche fallen to the grounde.' A fifth tower was on the south curtain, somewhere to the west of Scolland's Hall, presumably in the gap where the wall has fallen away, as no trace of it now exists. The sixth tower was that at the southwest angle, which still stands, and from here the survey follows the west curtain wall up to the great tower and the barbican wall to the outer gatehouse. After completing the circuit of the walls, the various buildings are visited, first the 'gret dongion' or great tower, then Scolland's Hall, the pantry, buttery and kitchen, the pastry, brewhouse, bakehouse and horse-mills; then the 'privie chamber above the hall' which is the solar at the east end; then the Gold Hole Tower, here called 'a litill toure at the baksyde of the same chambre, whiche hayth bene for draughtes to the saide chambre'; then the great chamber and chapel set against the east curtain next to the hall; then the large chapel at the south west 'in the castell garthe' with a chamber next to it. A reference to some 'decayde houses' ends the survey. The circuit of the walls is estimated at 2000ft (610m), and it is stated 'ther is no gonnys within the saide castell nor no artelire for the defence thereof.' The amount of material considered necessary for repairs is 161 roods of mason work, 630 oaks and 90 fothers of lead. There is nothing to show that any of the repairs advised were ever done, and Leland, whose visit must have taken place a few years afterwards, may be considered good evidence on the point.

The castle consists of three courts, the barbican or outer court, the great court and the cockpit. The great court is triangular, measuring 450ft (137m) from east to west along its base on the south, overlooking the River Swale, and 300ft (91m) from north to south, from the great tower to the south wall. On the southeast is the cockpit measuring 220ft (67m) from east to west by 170ft (52m) from north to south.

Barbican

Visitors enter the castle today over the site of the outer gatehouse, which is entirely destroyed. Parts, however, of the east walls of the barbican remain, and its extent is still preserved by the modern brick walls which enclose its area, following the lines of former stone walls. Projecting into the barbican on the south is the great tower or keep occupying the site and enclosing parts of the walls of the original eleventh-century gatehouse. The present inner gateway, with the rooms flanking it on either side, is modern, but occupies the place of the gateway cut in the curtain wall when the building of the great tower blocked the eleventh-century entrance to the castle. There was a portcullis here but apparently no drawbridge, and within the gate was a 'sware house' — that is, a square building, perhaps a two-storey gatehouse. The gate is set in the eleventh-century curtain wall to which a later upper part has been added.

The inner face of the curtain is here masked by modern buildings and a stairway leading up to the first floor of the great tower.

Keep

Passing through the gate, the great court of the castle is entered. To the right is the great tower or keep, 100ft 6in (30.6m) high. The fine arch on the ground floor opening to the courtyard is the inner archway of the eleventh-century gatehouse over which the keep is built. The ground storey of the tower has a stone vault dating from about 1330; the central pier from which it springs is, however, of the date of the keep, the second half of the twelfth century, and is built over a well, the arched opening to which may be seen. In the southwest corner a stone stair rises to the first floor. The usual entrance to a Norman keep was not on the ground floor but on the first floor, and Richmond follows the rule; the doorway is at the southeast, opening from the wall walk on the curtain wall, and another door on the southwest, now transformed into a window, formerly led to the wall at this point. The eleventh-century archway on the ground floor was probably blocked when the keep was built, but, if so, the blocking was removed many years ago.

The first-floor room is lighted by three windows on the north and has in the middle a round pillar standing over that on the ground floor and serving to support the floor beams of the room above. In the east and west walls are small vaulted chambers. The whole of the masonry was originally in squared ashlar, but much of this has been torn away, and the rubble walling which now replaces it is comparatively modern; the plan of the western wall chambers has been much altered in the process. The stairs from the first floor to the second ascend in the thickness of the south wall in a straight flight, having at their head a small lobby lighted by a widely splayed window, now reduced to a narrow slit.

The second floor has a fine room open to the roof and lighted from east and west; its ashlar facing is perfect except at the west. It has chambers in its east and west walls, as in the room below, but in more perfect condition, showing the original arrangement. In the eastern chambers are a few medieval graffiti.

From this floor another straight stair in the south and west walls leads to the battlements, which are known to have been repaired in the eighteenth century, but probably follow the original lines. There are two-storey turrets at each angle. From the wall walk can be seen the pitch of the original roof which, as usual in Norman keeps, was steeply gabled, but did not rise to the wall heads. At the head of the stair in the southwest angle are two wide splayed windows evidently intended to serve as an observation post like that on the floor below; there is also at the head of the stair in the west wall an oblique opening commanding the north wall walk.

Running southward from the keep is the east curtain wall of the great court, of eleventh-century date, and defended by three projecting towers, of which one has fallen. The first tower from the keep is the Robin Hood Tower, the name of the second, which has fallen, has not been preserved, and the third is the Gold Hole Tower, so named from a tradition of buried treasure.

Robin Hood Tower

The Robin Hood Tower, which according

The keep

to tradition was the prison of William the Lion in 1174, is of three storeys, the two lower, both barrel-vaulted, being of eleventh-century date, while the upper is a fourteenth-century addition. The ground storey is the chapel of St Nicholas and had had round its interior, except on the east, a wall arcade of semicircular arches and shafts with simple cushion capitals. At the east is a single narrow light, the flat sill of which seems to have held the mensa (table) of an altar, and on either side of the window are circular double-splayed openings, narrowest in the middle of the wall.

Adjoining the north side of the tower was a gateway through the eleventh-century curtain. Its jambs remain but the arch has fallen, and in the twelfth century it was blocked with masonry and two piers added on the inner face of the curtain. The space between them was probably spanned by an arch to carry the wall walk.

From the Robin Hood Tower to the north wall of the cockpit the curtain has been seriously damaged by the failure of its foundations.

The character of the eleventh-century masonry is well seen here, the occasional 'herringbone' courses being conspicuous. The facing is as a rule in large blocks, chiefly of the shaly rock on which the castle stands, and the ashlar dressing of the openings in the curtain are also in larger stones than those in the later Romanesque buildings in the castle. The shaly stone weathers badly and must have been often repaired in the course of years, the survey of 1538 noting that the outside of the 'seconde turret,' the tower now fallen, was at that time in decay. Evidences of such repair are plentiful in the patches of smaller masonry, and breaks in the coursing and the upper parts of the wall show that the parapets and wall walk belong to the early fourteenth-century work. The openings in the curtain at this point are, however, all of the early date and are doorways to garderobe chambers in the wall, or in one case to the stair leading to the fallen tower.

Further to the south along the wall is the group of ruined buildings of fourteenth-century date which can be identified from the 1538 survey as the great chamber and the chapel next to it. The buildings are of two storeys and the great chamber and chapel were on the upper floor. Next to the chapel on the north was a room called the chapel chamber, now destroyed. It was lighted by the two-light fourteenth-century window still to be seen in the curtain, and the holes for its floor joists remain in the chapel wall. The chapel was lighted only from the west by a window which the survey tells us was of three lights; there was a porch and a flight of steps leading up to the chapel, and these must have been on the west also, as their foundations show. Of the great chamber little can be said except that it was lighted from the west and had a fireplace in its west wall, like the room beneath it. In its north wall a small square opening gave a view into the chapel and in its south wall were three doors, one opening to the 'privy chamber' or solar at the east end of Scolland's Hall, and two to the hall itself.

Scolland's Hall

The hall takes its name from Scolland, sewer (steward) to the first earl, who held lands in Bedale. His successors, the Fitzalans of Bedale, had their station in the hall when performing their service of castle guard, and Scolland had doubtless owed the same service.

The hall is worthy of careful examination, as one of the earliest buildings of its class. It is a two-storey building, the ground floor being meant for cellars and storage. The east end of this floor is at a lower level than the rest, and was originally divided off by a cross wall. It has a wide eleventh-century arch in its north wall and must at first have served as an entrance lobby to the east gate; it is lighted on the south by two square-headed windows, also original.

The rest of the ground stage is entered through a lintelled doorway, and is lighted by five original square-headed windows on the south, which have below them on the outer face a row of beamholes, suggesting the existence of a wooden gallery here, but the windows are too narrow to have served as entrances to such a gallery. The keystones over the four eastern windows in this wall should be noted.

The hall itself was approached by an external stair at the northwest corner, leading up to a fine doorway of two orders with jambshafts, and a large roll-moulding

Scolland's Hall

on the inner order, returned in an unusual manner across the sill. Only in the outer arch does the masonry remain, and of the jambshafts one capital alone exists. This is of Corinthian character, and obviously early in style. The steps leading to this door from outside are represented by the masonry base which carried them.

The hall was lighted by two-light windows with round heads divided by a shaft with cushion capital. Three of these remain in the north wall, having lost their dividing shafts; a fourth, to the east of the other three, has been destroyed by the insertion of a doorway in the fourteenth century, and there may have been a fifth window at the northeast. On the south side are four similar two-light windows, and a fifth at the southeast has been superseded by a three-light fourteenth-century opening, intended to give more light to the upper or dais end of the hall than could be provided by the narrow two-light windows. On this south wall part of a twelfth-century arcaded cornice remains, and from differences in the masonry it seems clear that all the upper part of this wall, including the windows, is a rebuilding of the twelfth century, partly with the use of the old materials. At the west end there was originally one two-light window and a stair at the northwest angle, and there is nothing to suggest that any communication with a kitchen existed at first. The buildings to the west of the hall are of twelfth-century date, and at some subsequent time the sill of the west window has been cut down to serve as a doorway and openings broken out on either side of it giving the normal arrangement of the triple entrance to buttery, pantry and kitchen passage. From the sixteenth-century survey it is clear that the kitchen was not then in the twelfth-century buildings, but further west; no trace of a fireplace now to be seen.

The solar is at the east end of the hall over the arched entry from the cockpit and is itself in the lower part of its walls original eleventh-century work. In its south wall is an inserted two-light, thirteenth-century window, and over it the traces of the original gable end are to be seen. From the marks of fire on the early masonry it seems that the room was altered in the thirteenth century after being burnt out. It communicates with the hall by a door on the west and in its east wall are a fireplace, a single trefoiled window of fourteenth-century date, and a square-headed doorway, apparently original, which must have opened to an external wooden gallery like that on the south side of Scolland's Hall. The beamholes still exist on the east face, and there is some evidence of an opening in the south wall of the adjoining Gold Hole Tower which would have led to the gallery.

Gold Hole Tower

The Gold Hole Tower contained the garderobes or latrines of the castle; the lower part is eleventh-century work, including the garderobe pits and remains of the arch which spanned them; the upper part is a rebuilding of the early fourteenth century and contains a room with fireplace and garderobe entered from the wall walk.

Cockpit

The cockpit or second court is entered through the basement of Scolland's Hall. It is a roughly triangular court sloping eastwards and was enclosed with masonry walls late in the twelfth century. Of this work the north wall remains in great part, with a wide archway at the northwest, but the rest is mostly fallen, including the two towers which once stood at the east and south of the court. Through the northwest archway the east side of the castle, with the remains of the fallen tower and the buttresses added to support the east curtain wall, may be seen. The battered base of the Robin Hood Tower with the gable enclosing the windows of St Nicholas Chapel is notable, and immediately to the north of the tower is a recess containing part of the jambs of a destroyed gateway of the eleventh century.

Returning through Scolland's Hall, the remains of the buildings on the south of the great court, overlooking the Swale, may be seen. They are much ruined and can only be identified conjecturally from the survey. The details show that they are of the twelfth and thirteenth centuries. In addition to a wall tower which stood where the gap in the curtain now occurs, the kitchen, brewhouse and other offices occupied this side of the castle.

At the southwest angle is a small tower, partly of original date with a later top, and from this point the early curtain wall stands to a considerable height with a lot of herringbone masonry. In it is a tall and wide arch marking the west end of the greater chapel of the castle, and beneath it is an eleventh-century archway.

Gold Hole Tower, seen through the gateway to the Cockpit

Glossary

ARCADE	Passage arched over; covered walk; series of arches on the same plane; range of arches carried on piers
ASHLAR	Squared block(s) of stone; masonry constructed of this
BAILEY	Walled enclosure or courtyard in a castle
BARBICAN	Outward extension of a gateway, protecting it
BARREL VAULT	Vault with semi-cylindrical roof; arched roof or ceiling unbroken by cross-vaults
BATTERED	With the base or ground courses sloped
BATTLEMENT	Indented parapet; parapet and enclosed roof
BUTTRESS	Masonry built against a wall to give it additional strength
CORNICE	Projection near the top of a wall; ornamental carved moulding
CURTAIN	Wall enclosing a courtyard; portion of a rampart which connects two adjacent bastions
DAIS	Low platform for principal table
DRAWBRIDGE	Wooden bridge which can be raised towards a gateway by means of chains or ropes attached to its outer end
GARDEROBE	Latrine or privy
KEEP	Great tower or donjon, normally used of eleventh- and twelfth-century buildings but sometimes applied loosely to those of later date
KEYSTONE	Middle stone in an arch
MOTTE	Castle mound of earth or turf (eleventh and twelfth centuries)
PALISADE	Palings of strong timber
PARAPET	Screen on the terreplein (surface or rampart behind parapet, where guns are mounted) covering troops and guns from the enemy's observation and fire
PORTCULLIS	Iron-shod wooden grill suspended by chains in grooves in front of a gate, and let down to ground level in times of attack
SOLAR	Private room of the owner and his family, adjacent to the hall
TREFOILED	Three-leaved
VAULT	Ceiling of flat stone slabs or continuous arch of stone or brick; arched stone roof